MARTIAL ARTS AROUND THE WORLD

BY JOHN STEVEN SOET

ISBN: 0-86568-151-1

LIBRARY OF CONGRESS CATALOG NUMBER: 91-065259

Designed by: Danilo J. Silverio

 **UNIQUE PUBLICATIONS**

4201 Vanowen Place Burbank, CA 91505

TABLE OF CONTENTS

INTROD

The term "martial" means "warlike." It takes its name from Mars, the Roman god of war. Unfortunately, nature provides for survival of the fittest. We live on a planet where various species survive by preying on other species. More often than not, in nature, animals meet violent deaths.

Nature has also provided animals with various defense systems. In some animals, skin coloration blends the creature in with nature, creating a biological form of camouflage. In creatures such as the skunk, the ability to emit a pungent

odor combined with readily identifiable markings (white stripes on black fur) is one of the most ingenious self-defense systems ever devised.

In creatures not so blessed, however, body systems originally designed for another purpose must be used for defense against predators. A dog, for example, cannot stand on his feet and punch out an adversary, so the canine relies on the teeth used to chew food as a primary weapon. The feline species (cat family) relies on the bite, as well as the claws provided by nature to climb and hold objects.

UCTION

The Mixed Blessing of Humanity

The human race, of course, is unique among species. Proportionally one of the weakest mammals, off-balance compared to four-legged creatures, and lacking in natural defense systems such as hard shells or sharp claws, the human being must rely on a superior reasoning capacity to prevail against aggressors.

While world peace is a worthwhile goal, it has never been possible. Since the biblical story of Cain slaying Abel, our history has been a red-and-white checkerboard of bloodshed. On the smaller scale, there have always been those ready to prey upon others for assorted reasons. Sometimes the reasons are purely psychological in origin — one simply may not like another person. Some-

times an individual may seek to take something away from another, such as property. More often than not, human aggression has been motivated by fear — the aggressor feels threatened by another and acts to remove the threat.

With a few minor zoological exceptions, the human is also unique in the ability to fashion weapons of attack and defense. The stick and rock were probably the first weapons, followed by large clubs, crude flint knives, and nuclear fusion devices. The human is a wily creature, and when no weapons were available,

people would soon devise ways of using the materials at hand, such as farming implements, as weapons (plowshares beaten into swords, so to speak).

Early Attempts at Weapons Control

From the beginning, those in authority have always sought to keep weapons out of the hands of their subjects. This has always been misrepresented, since the first tribal chief decided to lock up the spears, as being for the protection of the people. In reality, weapons control and regulation has always been for the purpose of disarming subordinates and, therefore, making them easier to control. Virtually every society which voluntarily submitted to weapons control in 7,000-plus years of recorded history has fallen victim to tyranny.

However, human beings are also unique in the desire to be free, and to not submit to the authority of others. What child, when reading a sign saying "keep off the grass," can  resist walking on a fresh green lawn?

Therefore, during repressive periods in history, human ingenuity made itself felt. Methods were devised for fashioning weapons out of innocent objects and ingenious empty-hand systems were developed. From hidden Philippine campfires during the Spanish occupation to Okinawan beaches during the time of the Japanese conquest, from territorial Hawaii to Taoist monasteries, people

made fighting and self-defense an art form.

Various methods were developed for practicing these arts. Often, the training would be through the learning of intricate forms resembling dances (popularly known by their Japanese name, "kata"). Thousands of repetitions would literally reprogram the subconscious mind so reaction to a threat would be spontaneous. Often, the training would be more direct one-on-one sparring. In some cultures, matches were fought to the death.

The Two Main Theories

There are two main theories as to the origins of today's martial arts. The first is the more exciting but more flawed *common origin theory.* This theory traces a rather fanciful history of the arts.

Originally the arts were supposed to have originated in one of two places — India or Ancient Greece. The Greek theory holds that Alexander's troops brought Olympic style fighting, *pankration*, to India. The Indian theory is simply based on the fact that there were many sophisticated martial arts forms, such as *kaliripiyat* being practiced in ancient parts of India.

It is then said that Bodhidharma (Tamo in Japanese), a Buddhist monk, crossed the Himalayas and built the Shaolin Temple in the Hunan province. Bodhidharma, alarmed at the monks' terrible physical condition, taught them several postures, based on the knowledge he acquired in India, which became the basis for Chinese martial arts (chuan-fa or "fist way," often misread as "kung-fu" or "something done well").

The popular tradition then holds that during the destruction of the temple many centuries later, the monks taught their art to the public, and it eventually spread through Southeast Asia (Indonesia, Thailand and the Philippines). At the same time, Okinawan fisherman journeyed to China and learned the art and brought it back to their island chain.

As historically romantic as this story is, it is highly unlikely that it happened that way. First, we now know that the Shaolin temple was standing centuries before Bodhidharma's arrival. Second, figurines of Chinese warriors have been discovered in martial arts forms poses which predate this very same arrival by more than five hundred years.

It is much more likely that the arts were developed by the military. Quite often, upon retiring, soldiers would take up the monastic life. Often, when a new dynasty came to power, soldiers from the old dynasty would be declared wanted criminals, and take refuge in the temples. Most probably, they pooled their knowledge and evolved new and more sophisticated techniques.

The second theory of martial evolution is the independent evolution theory. This theory, basically, holds that the human body can only move so many ways and there are a finite number of ways to do things right. Therefore, in spite of certain similarities, independent development of styles makes sense. This can readily be evidenced in the similarities between the kicks of French savate and Northern-style kung-fu, in spite of the fact that many of the savate moves were developed centuries before Europe had any great degree of contact with China.

Regardless of historical theory, recent history proves that the demands of time and terrain cause an art to evolve. Each and every culture has changed arts to which it has been exposed to suit its own unique needs. Okinawans turned kung-fu into a harder, more powerful striking system, while William Chow's kenpo, developed in the then-lawless Hawaiian territory, had to contend with attacks from knives and firearms. The arts of the Philippines had to deal with varying types of terrain, such as slippery marshes, tall grass, and firm sand. Indonesian tribes expected attacks at any moment, so ingenious defenses against multiple attackers were developed. And such a recent development as Israeli martial arts actually contains techniques for dealing with live hand grenades!

The Focus of this Book

This book is not meant to be a historical dissertation on every martial art in the world. It is intended to serve as a comparative guide to the martial strategies and techniques of various nations.

It is vital to point out that the photographs contained herein are nothing more than elements of frozen time. It is impossible to depict certain other attributes which make a technique effective. A technique which looks simplistic, for example, may have been executed, in reality, with blinding speed. Techniques against multiple opponents can also be tricky to interpret because they don't depict such subtleties as weight shifting. And, above all, the most important attribute of all, timing, is something which simply cannot be captured on film.

Every day, ancient knowledge is both forgotten and rediscovered. Long-forgotten interpretations of ancient forms are discerned, and new and different applications of techniques are developed to deal with changing times.

Up until a mere hundred years ago, anyone fortunate enough to be able to study a martial art was generally bound to one style. One instructor taught in the village, and the local or national style was all that was available.

Today, we have the technology to view human history through combative strategies. We have the unprecedented opportunity to make side-by-side comparisons and witness new styles evolve.

AFRICA

RE-EFI AREH-EHSEE

Cradle of civilization, all human beings have African roots. Sophisticated civilizations rose and fell in Africa long before the first homo sapiens left the continent.

One unique and devastating African martial art is the art known as re-efi areh-ehsee, which comes from Etrirea, in northeast Africa (modern Ethiopia). In many ways, it resembles Indonesian silat, but the historical records are so inconsistent it would be pointless to speculate on the reasons for the similarities.

The art of capoeira (see the "South America" section) is based on an African martial art. There are other theories which contend that African martial arts were the first refined fighting systems in history.

Dennis Newsome is one of the world's leading authorities on jailhouse rock and African martial arts.

1) Dennis Newsome traps the attacker's kicking leg while rushing in with an elbow strike. 2) He maintains his hold on the leg, kneeing his attacker in the groin. 3) He follows this with a headbutt to the face. 4) He elbows the attacker in the face as he pulls back on the leg, executing a takedown. 5) He can now finish his helpless attacker.

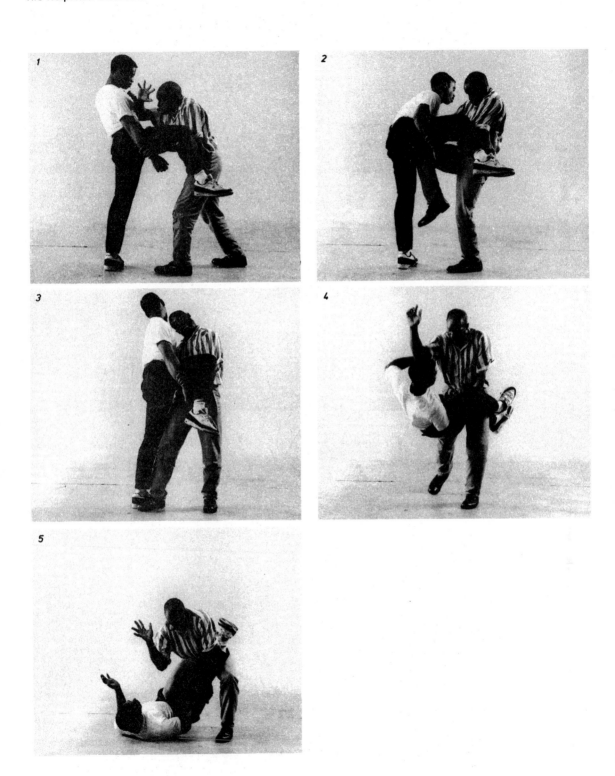

1) Dennis Newsome is pinned in a tight bear hug. 2) To break the grip, he thrusts his hips back hard. 3) His opponent now off-balanced, Dennis twists sideways and hits him in the groin. 4) This is followed with a headbutt to the face. 5) Dennis can now execute a hip throw, lifting his attacker up and over. 6) On the ground, the attacker is easy prey for Dennis' armlock.

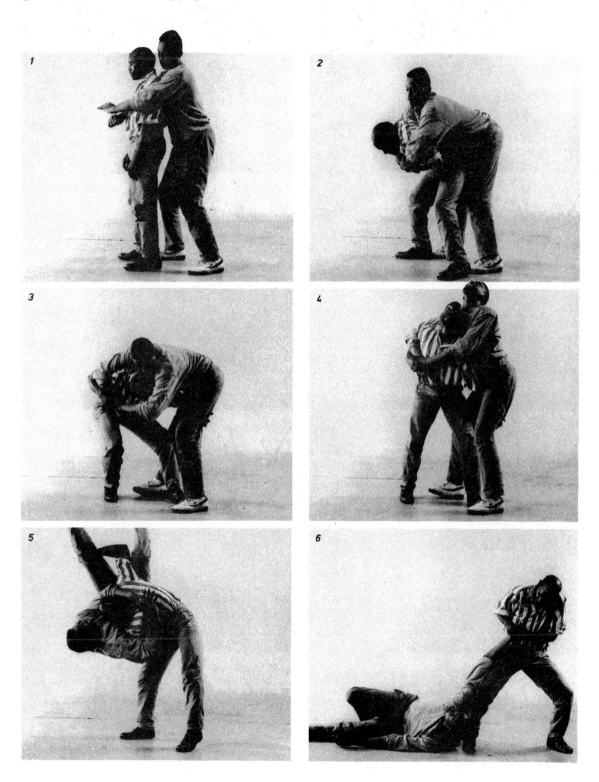

1) Dennis Newsome is grabbed in a "regulation" choke. 2) He grabs his attacker's arm and twists his body completely around. 3) He frees himself, continuing to apply the armlock. 4) He takes the attacker down. 5) Dennis goes down with the attacker and lands on his head with his knee.

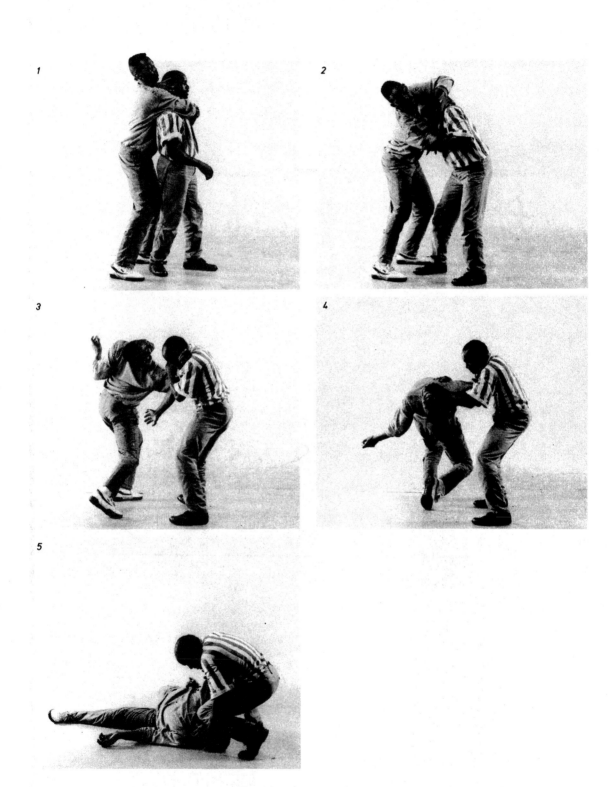

BRAZIL

CAPOEIRA

Characterized by intricate acrobatic moves, capoeira (cah poe eye rah) originated in Africa, and was developed and refined by the Black slave community of Brazil. As it was illegal for slaves to practice martial arts, it was practiced in clandestine sessions and the slaves trained to music, disguising the brutally-effective moves as dance. After emancipation, capoeira academies began to flourish throughout Brazil, and now this art is spreading to the rest of the world.

Cedric Adams is a student of capoeira and film choreographer from Los Angeles, California.

1) Cedric Adams is menaced by an attacker. 2) As the attacker punches, Cedric steps out of the way of the punch and deflects the fist. 3) He deflects the fist off to the side. 4) Cedric now uses his momentum to begin a handstand. 5) He thrusts his feet up into the air, balancing on his hand. 6) The attacker is finished by a full-power kick to the face.

1) Cedric Adams faces his attacker. 2) As the attacker kicks, Cedric remains still. 3) At the last instant, he simply angles his body out of the way. 4) He stretches out his foot between the base of the opponent's legs. 5) The opponent is swept off of his support leg by Cedric's sweep. 6) Cedric finishes the fight with an elbow to the head.

1) Cedric Adams finds his arms pinned to the side by an unseen attacker. 2) He grabs the attacker's hands holding them hard, as he steps out sideways in a low, wide stance. 3) He simply leans forward, low, at the waist. His attacker must go with him or lose his grip. 4) Quickly, Cedric reaches down with his hands. 5) He grabs his opponent's leg and pulls him to the floor. 6) Supported on his hands, Cedric launches a powerful rearward kick into his now downed opponent.

BRAZIL

GRACIE JIU-JITSU

Brazil, in many ways, is a mirror image of the United States of America, its neighbor to the north. An ethnic melting pot, many Asian immigrants settled in Brazil. Carlos and Helio Gracie learned traditional jujutsu from a Japanese nobleman, and developed Gracie jiu-jitsu, a unique martial art which has been tested against other arts and remained undefeated for 60 years.

The Gracie brothers are the world's leading proponents of Gracie jiu-jitsu, a style which has gone undefeated for nearly 65 years.

1) Renzo Gracie faces off with Rickson Gracie. 2) Renzo throws his punch and Rickson deflects. 3) Rickson ducks under and grabs Renzo by the waist. 4) Lifting him up, Rickson initiates a throw. 5) Renzo hits the ground hard. 6) He is now vulnerable to Rickson's follow-up attack.

1) Royce and Rilion square off. 2) Royce throws a front kick. 3) Rilion deflects the kick and hooks his arm under the kicking leg. 4) Rilion sweeps Royce's supporting leg, throwing him to the ground. 5) He finishes with an armlock.

1) Carlos does not see Rolker sneaking up from behind. 2) Rolker grabs Carlos around the throat to choke him out. 3) Carlos immediately grabs Rolker's arm with both hands and pivots on his right foot. 4) This allows him to regain his balance, and relieves the pressure of the choke. 5) Carlos uses the momentum of his spin to throw Rolker. 6) On the ground, Rolker is easy prey for Carlos' punch.

1) The aggressor (Royce Gracie) approaches the defender (Renzo Gracie). 2) He grabs him by the neck. 3) Renzo falls backward, placing one foot on Royce's hip. 4) This motion lifts Royce up. 5) Renzo spins Royce around with his foot applying an armlock. 6) On the ground, Royce is overcome by Renzo's armlock.

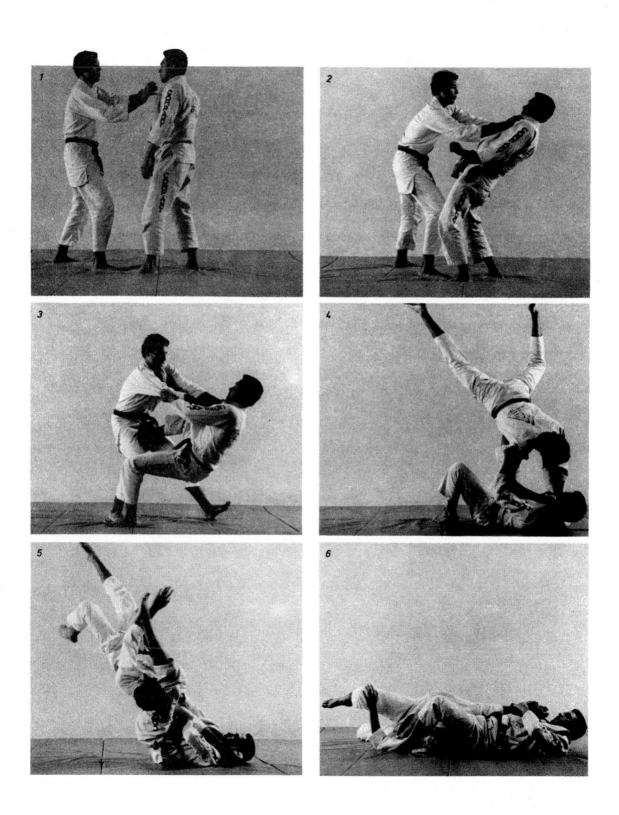

CHINA

PRAYING MANTIS

The praying mantis system was developed by Wong Long in the 16th century. Wong Long was already proficient in several systems of kung-fu when he was badly beaten by an adversary. As he was licking his wounds, he observed a praying mantis battling another insect, and how direct and effective the moves were. He incorporated the moves of the mantis, along with the footwork from monkey style, and formed a new combative art.

Scott Cohen is a certified sifu of Tai Chi Praying Mantis under Sifu Kam Yuen.

1) Scott Cohen, a certified sifu under Kam Yuen, faces an attack. 2) Scott deftly steps to the side, clearing himself of the path of the punch, and traps the punching hand with a palm-up deflection. 3) He steps around, twisting, and forces the attacking arm down in a painful lock. 4) Following-through, Scott smashes his opponent in the face with his elbow. 5) He extends his arm, pulling back, and throws out a foot, sweeping his opponent. 6) The opponent is now neutralized, and helpless against any further attacks.

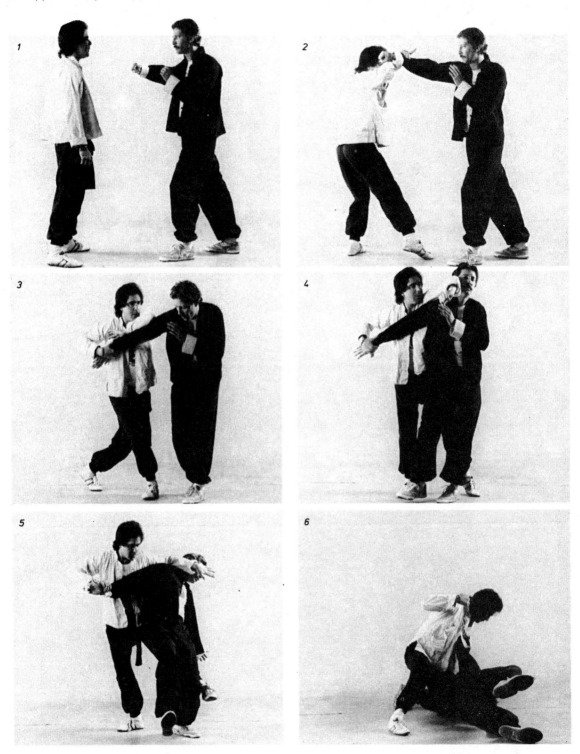

The instant Scott is grabbed, he is in motion (1), twisting free of his attackers and grabbing the first attacker by the head (2). He sweeps him into the second attacker (3), and pivots (4), which brings the two men down (5), in a tangle of arms and legs (6).

1) Scott Cohen, a certified instructor under Sifu Kam Yuen, is faced with an attack. 2) As his attacker kicks, Scott blocks the kick with his leg. 3) Scott whips a backfist into the attacker's temple as he steps down. 4) From this point, he steps around, twisting, and elbows the attacker in the other temple. 5) He wraps his arm around the attacker, applying a headlock, and bends him down, exposing his back. 6) An elbow strike to the tailbone finishes the attacker.

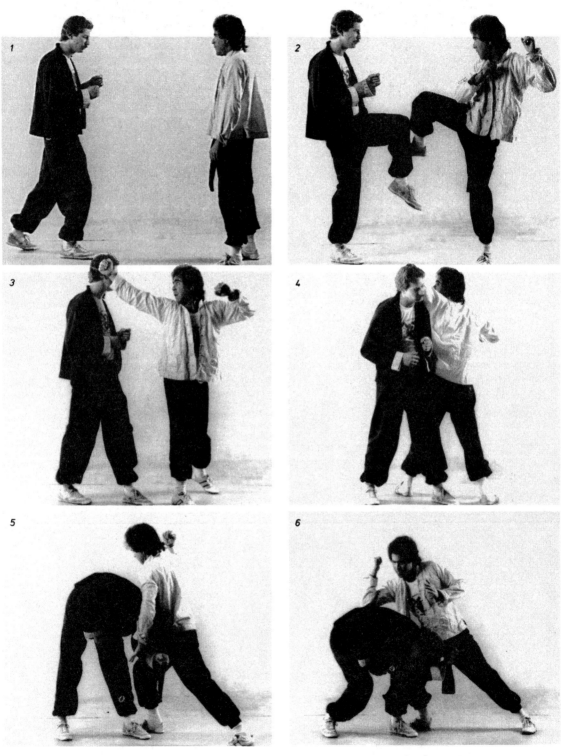

1) Sifu Scott Cohen is about to be grabbed. 2) He grabs his attacker's wrists and drops into a low crouch. 3) From this point, he pulls the opponent down with his bodyweight, and rolls onto his back. 4) He hooks his legs around the outside of the opponent's legs, and simply rocks forward, pulling him to the ground. 5) On the ground, he pins the opponent's leg and chambers his kick. 6) The opponent is finished by a kick to the jaw.

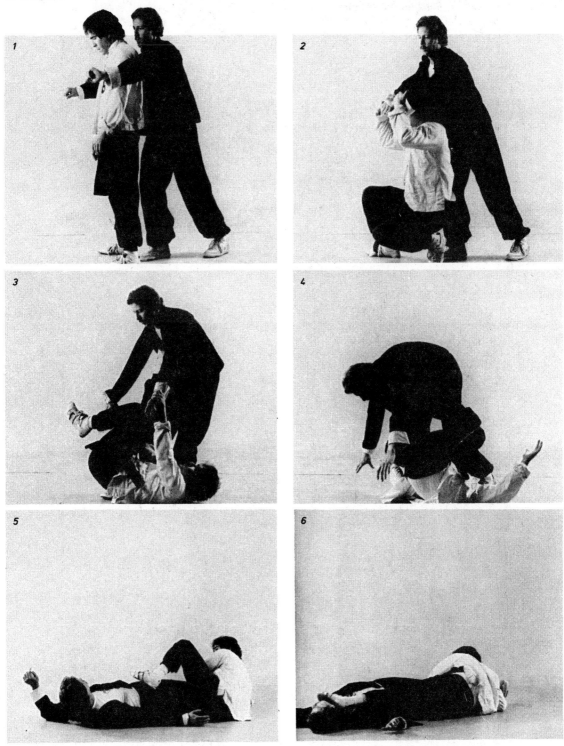

CHINA

WING CHUN

Wing chun (also spelled ving tsun) kung-fu is said to have been formulated in the 17th century by the Shaolin nun Ng Mui. Ng Mui, from the Fukien monastery, encountered young Yimm Wing Chun, a local girl who was being forced to marry the village bully. Ng Mui and Wing Chun developed a springy, simplified direct style based on energy, which enabled Wing Chun to defeat the bully. The effectiveness of this art makes it one of the most popular kung-fu styles in the world.

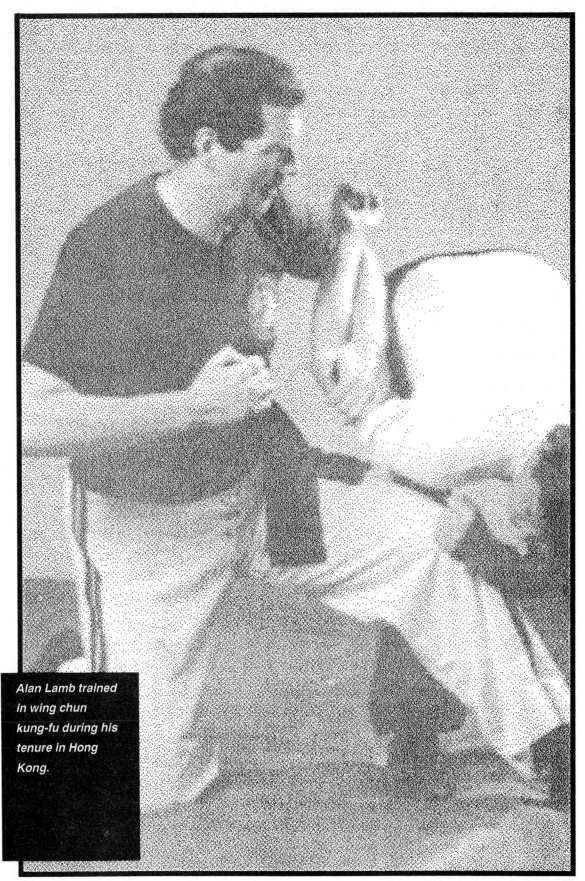

Alan Lamb trained in wing chun kung-fu during his tenure in Hong Kong.

1) Alan Lamb finds himself in a choke which could render him unconscious in seconds. 2) Alan grabs his opponent's hands, pivots and drives his elbow into his attacker's ribs, hard. 3) As he strikes, he drops to his knee and breaks the hold. 4) Alan then applies an armlock and cocks back his free hand to deliver a punch to the attacker's head.

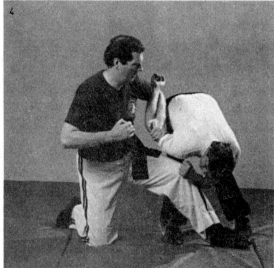

1) Wing chun instructor Alan Lamb immediately applies the trapping principle by kicking up to his attacker's elbow and pushing his arm back. 2) Alan then whips his leg around to the opponent's knee and yanks backward on it. 3) This motion sweeps the opponent's leg and throws him to the ground, hard. 4) Alan rolls over onto his opponent and grabs the back of his head to push the attacker's face into the ground.

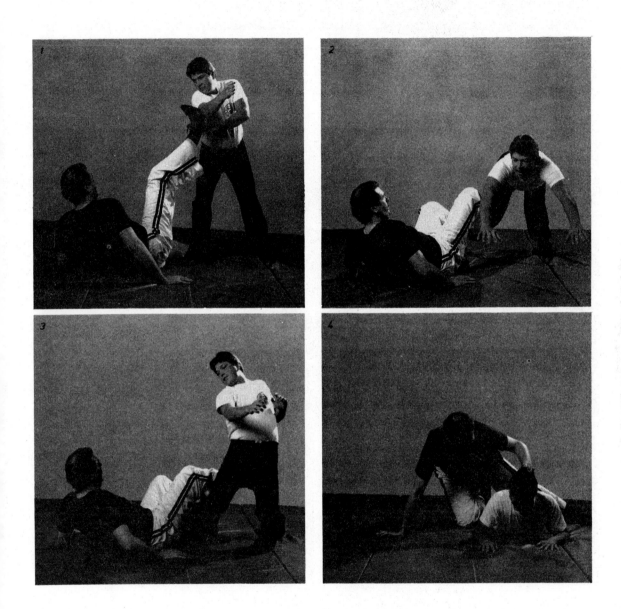

FRANCE

SAVATE

European history is battle scarred. A small continent of mixed cultures and nationalities, many fighting styles were developed, from the Welsh cornu breton to Spanish saber fencing. The knight of the middle ages was the equivalent of Japan's samurai.

Although many European nations have various boxing and wrestling styles, and there are those scholars who contend that Greek pankration might just be the forerunner of all martial arts, the French art of savate is the most well-known form of European unarmed combat. Savate developed in the streets of France, and true savate, unlike the sport boxe francaise, incorporates grappling and throwing with striking moves.

Other arts of Europe: Catchascatchcan Wrestling, Cornu Breton, English Boxing, Italian Fencing, Sambo (Russia) and Spanish Saber (Escrima).

Salem Assli is a silver glove instructor of French savate.

Salem Assli's opponent appears nonaggressive (1), but suddenly launches a sucker punch, which Salem parries (2). Salem pulls the attacker into a head butt (3), knees him in the midsection (4), and uses his kicking leg to sweep him (5). On the way down, the attacker is finished-off with an elbow strike (6).

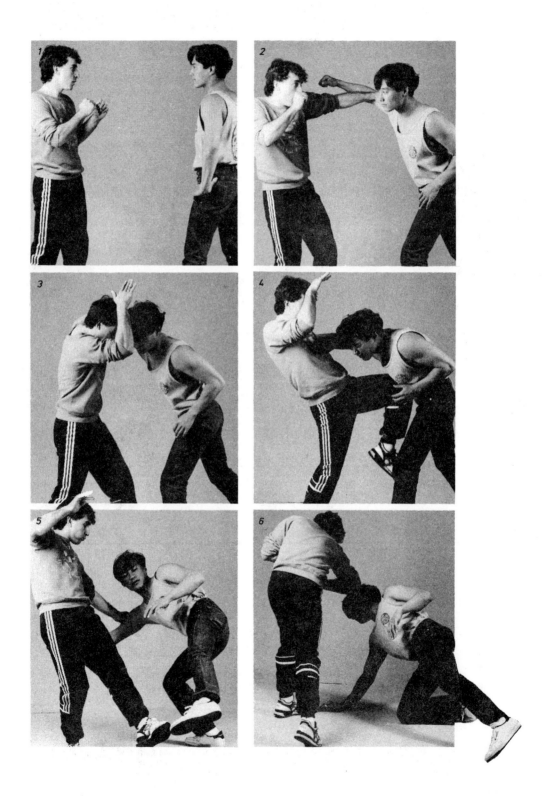

Salem faces an attacker who brandishes a stick (1) As he swings, Salem bobs to the side and punches him (2). He follows though with a roundhouse kick (3), and brings his foot around to the attacker's outside knee (4). All he need do is step forward (5), to bring him down (6).

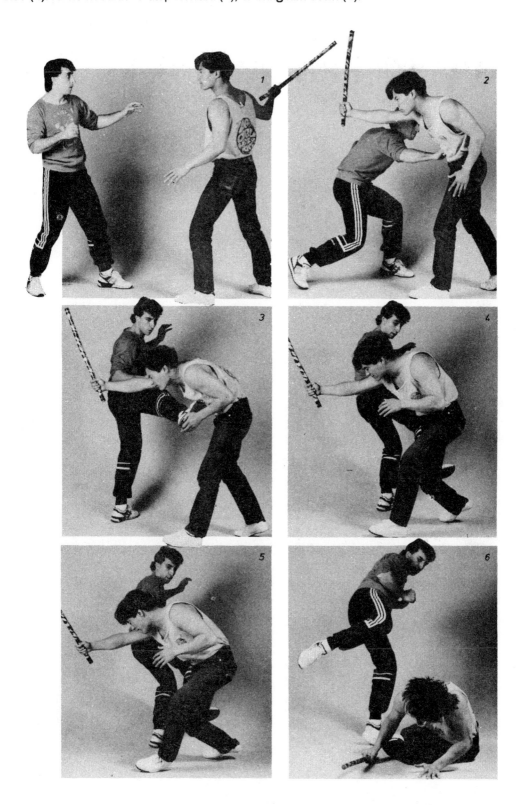

Salem faces his attacker and sees the knife (1). As the attacker begins to thrust, Salem positions his defense (2). He guides the knife past his body (3), kicks to the thigh (4), then pushes on the opponent's support leg while pulling on his wrist (5). He then spins and knees his opponent's face (6).

Salem faces off with his opponent (1), who starts to move, and Salem raises his leg to allow himself to kick or block with it (2). As the attacker completes his kick, Salem elects to block (3), then leans forward, snapping into the groin (4). He then grabs the attacker's hair (5), and knees his face (6).

FRANCE

BOXE FRANCAISE

Boxe Francaise is the sport aspect of original French savate. Whereas street savate is very brutal, and includes groin kicks, nerve strikes, throws and eye gouges, boxe francaise techniques are limited to those which are "ring legal." Nevertheless, the devastating speed and flexibility of this art makes boxe francaise competitors second to none.

Paul Vunak is a certified instructor of savate under Daniel Duby, and a full instructor of jeet kune do concepts.

1) Daniel Duby and Paul Vunak face each other in a demonstration of the sporting aspect of French savate (boxe Francaise). 2) As Daniel shoots out a right cross, Paul angles out to the side, evading the blow. 3) Paul is now able to fire a right into Daniel's exposed midsection

1) Paul Vunak, head of Progressive Fighting Systems, bends down and thrusts back as he grabs his attacker's hands. 2) He throws his body to the left, dragging his attacker off balance. 3) During the throwing process, Paul twists so his attacker will land on the ground. 4) Paul lands on the attacker hard and thrusts his head back into his attacker's face.

1) Paul Vunak's attacker chokes. 2) Paul grabs the attackers arm to relieve the pressure and bites the arm, hard. 3) Now that he is free, Paul pivots around and blasts his attacker with an elbow to the face. 4) He then administers the coup de grace, a palm strike to the face.

1) Paul Vunak, a certified savate instructor as well as an instructor of jeet kune do concepts, cocks back his leg as his opponent moves in for the kill. 2) Paul kicks up to the groin. At the same time, he places his left foot against his attacker's ankle. 3) He then brings his right foot behind his attacker's leg and kicks the back of his knee, bringing him down. 4) On the ground, Paul levers the opponent's leg, applying upward pressure with his left leg; downward pressure with his right leg

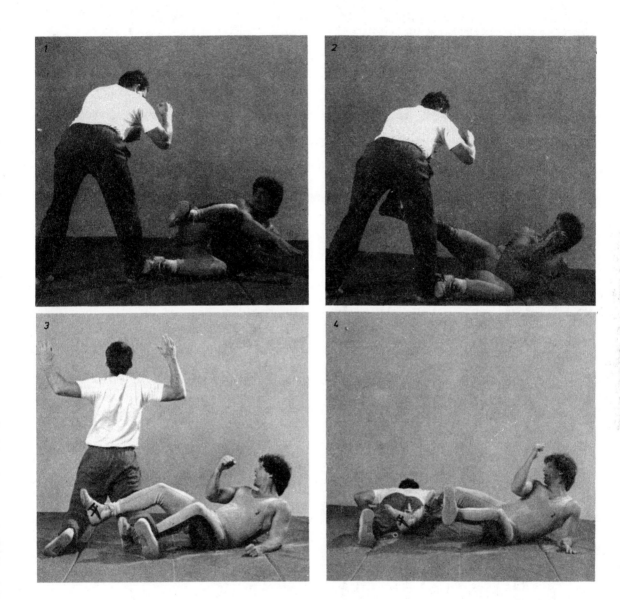

INDONESIA

PENTJAK SILAT

The Indonesian archipelago developed one of the most sophisticated martial arts systems the world has ever known—pentjak silat (pent jack see lot). Although its origins can only be speculated upon, the Indonesians believe that most arts originated in India, and spread north into China and south to Indonesia. Silat is one of the most complete martial arts systems ever devised.

Specific styles of Silat: kara-Ton (Royal style), Serah (Badui style), Soetji Hati ("Heart" style), Tji Kalong ("Bat" style) and Tjimande (River style).

Rudy Ter Linden is an instructor of four different styles of pentjak silat — serah, soetji hati, tji kalong and tjimande. He is considered the foremost authority on silat in the United States.

Rudy Ter Linden faces a noncholant-looking bystander (1), who makes a sudden move, which Rudy instantly intercepts (2). Rudy continues his instant response, stepping behind his attacker (3), turning and elbowing the attacker's face (4), which sweeps him to the ground (5). Rudy then steps around and applies an armlock/neck break (6). This entire move was so rapid and instantly responsive it could not be timed.

Rudy faces an unknown adversary (1). His opponent suddenly kicks, but the instant he moves, Rudy angles and grabs the leg while hitting the throat with his arm (2). He then uses the "push-pull principle" to throw his opponent (3). The camera angle is reversed so the reader can get the proper positioning (4). A slight twist of the hips and the attacker is down (5), and Rudy applies an armlock and drops on his throat (6). Like most silat moves, this appeared instantaneous.

Rudy is taken by surprise (1), as his bag is grabbed (2). He instantly whips his arm around the attacker's neck (3), twists his body around (4), drops the attacker into a neck break (5), and chokes him out (6).

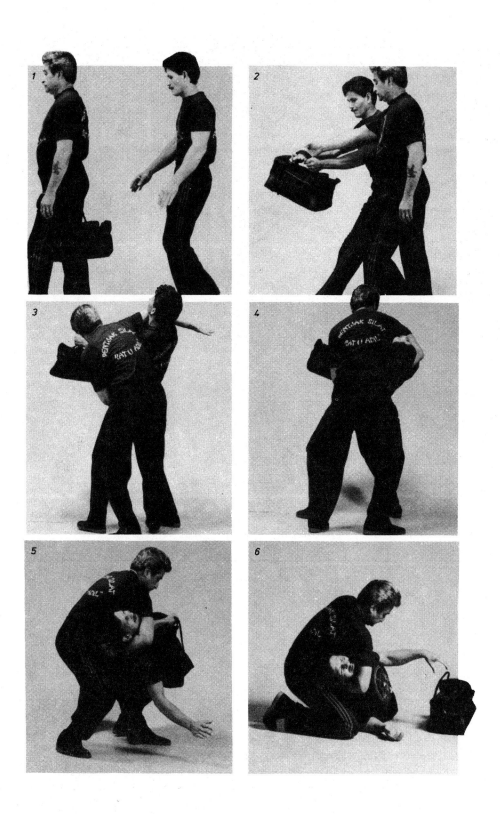

As the attacker swings his stick, Rudy angles to the side (1), catches his wrist, and applies an armlock (2). Rudy then steps in and brings his arm across the attacker's face (3) and pulls him around (4). Rudy pulls him to the ground (5), where he applies an armlock/neck break.

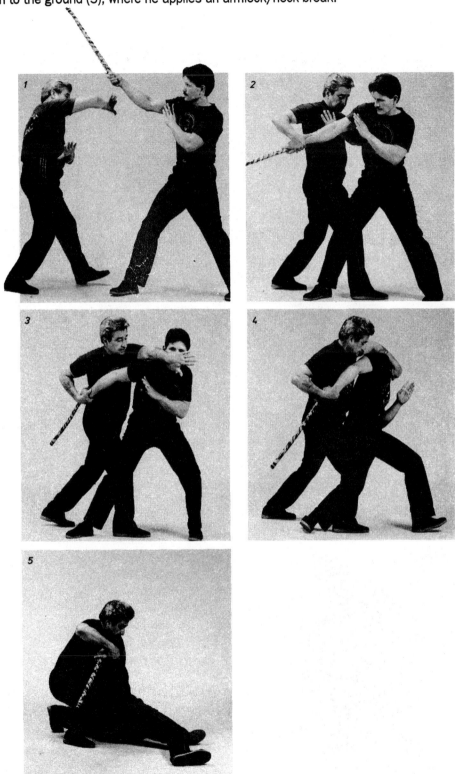

Rudy begins a conversation, unaware of the hidden knife (1). As the attacker thrusts the knife, Rudy responds subconsciously, due to years of practicing silat's unique djurus, and launches into the following sequence, performed in one fluid motion (2): he traps the elbow of the other arm, effectively neutralizing his attacker's weapons (3), turns at the waist, pushing with his right arm and shoulder while stepping through (4), continues to twist around, hooking the foot (not shown) and downing the opponent (5), and renders him helpless on the ground (6).

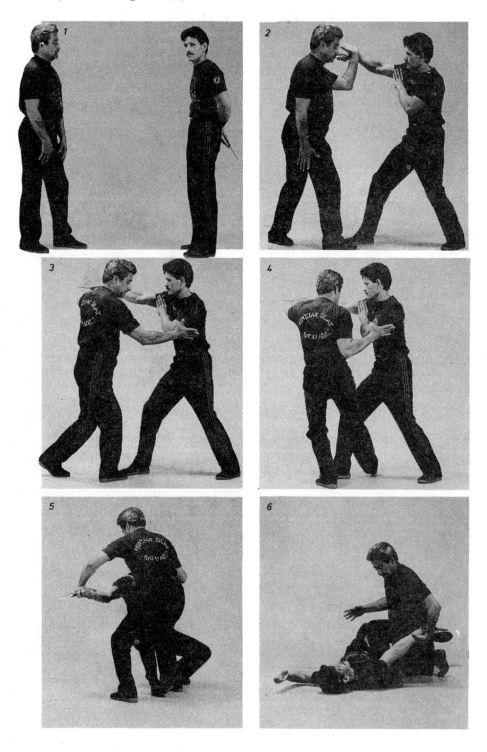

Rudy is grabbed (1). He immediately twists his body all the way around (2), bringing one arm up over his head. He then steps between an attacker's feet (3), and pulls both attackers into a sweep (4). The attackers go down (5), where they are vulnerable to a counterattack (6).

ISRAEL

HISARDUT

Hisardut is one of the most modern arts featured in this work. It was developed in the war-torn Middle East to be the Israeli's last line of defense. It was founded by Dennis Hanover, who had trained in judo, kyokushinkai karate and jujutsu, to cope with modern self-defense needs. Techniques such as knocking soldiers off of horses were discarded in favor of such techniques as defending against a thrown hand grenade. Hisardut is a complete art, dealing with all ranges and zones.

Alon Stiovi is a fourth dan instructor of Hisardut, and the leader of the system in the United States of America.

Against an attack from behind. Alon doesn't see Ofer Lavi sneaking up on him (1). As Ofer applies a bear hug (2), Alon immediately steps out to his sides, dropping into a stance resembling the classic "horse," and brings up his arms, breaking the hold (3). Trapping Ofer's arm, Alon delivers an elbow strike (4), reaches down and grabs his foot (5), and pulls forward, bringing him to the ground (6).

Against a kick. Alon faces Ofer (1). As Ofer tries a front kick, Alon jams (2) and counters with a low-line kick to the thigh (3). He then follows up (4) and delivers a roundhouse to the head (5&6).

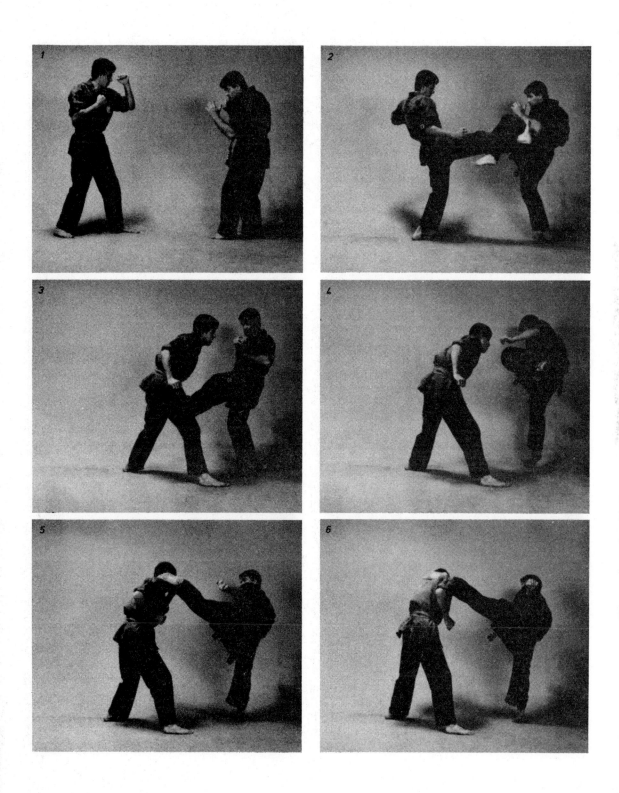

Against a sneak choke. Alon is looking the other way (1) when Ofer Lavi grabs him in a choke (2). He gets Alon in a headlock (3), and Alon reaches up to relieve the pressure (4). Alon then fires a shot to the jaw (5), and the groin (6). He lifts the stunned Ofer up (7), and drops to the ground, breaking his back over his knee (8).

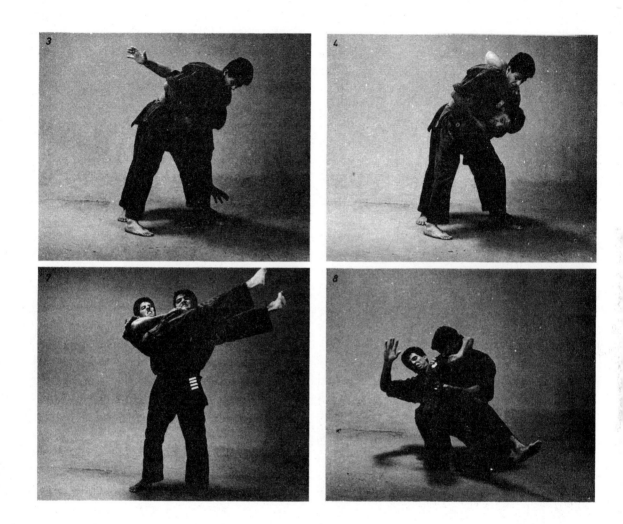

Against a frontal choke. Alon faces off with Shalom Shadev (1). Shalom reaches out and attempts to strangle him (2). Alon brings his arms straight up and out (3), breaking the hold, and delivers a double shuto to both carotid arteries (4). He then yanks Shalom's head down and headbutts him (5), knees him to the midsection (6), takes him down (7), and finishes with an elbow to the base of the skull (8).

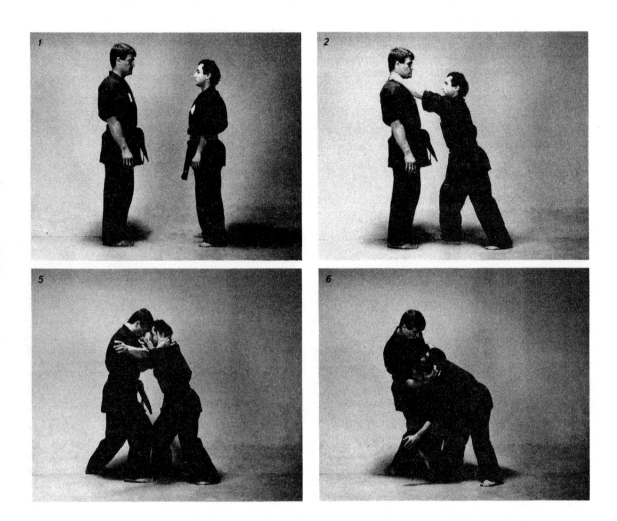

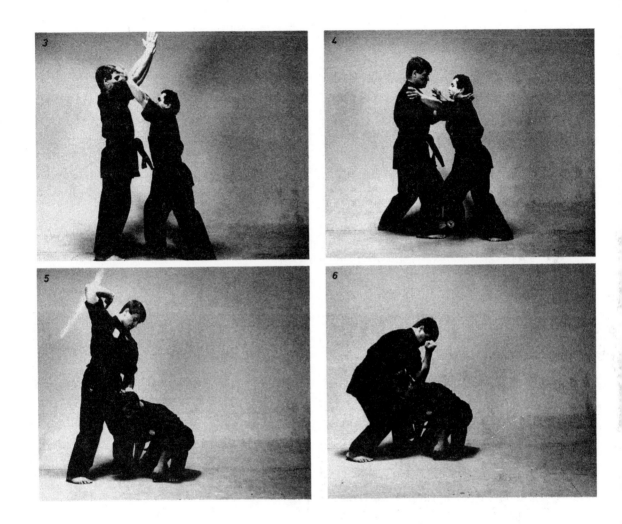

Against a two-man attack. Alon faces his attackers (1), and Ofer applies a full-nelson while Shalom draws a knife (2). Alon drops to loosen the pressure of the hold (3), and does a combination low side kick to the knife hand (4) and a high side kick to the throat (5) of Shalom. He then leans forward, off-balancing Ofer (6), then flings himself back (7), and lands on him (8). On the ground he chambers an elbow (9) and finishes him (10). These last two moves are shown from the reverse angle for correct technique (11&12).

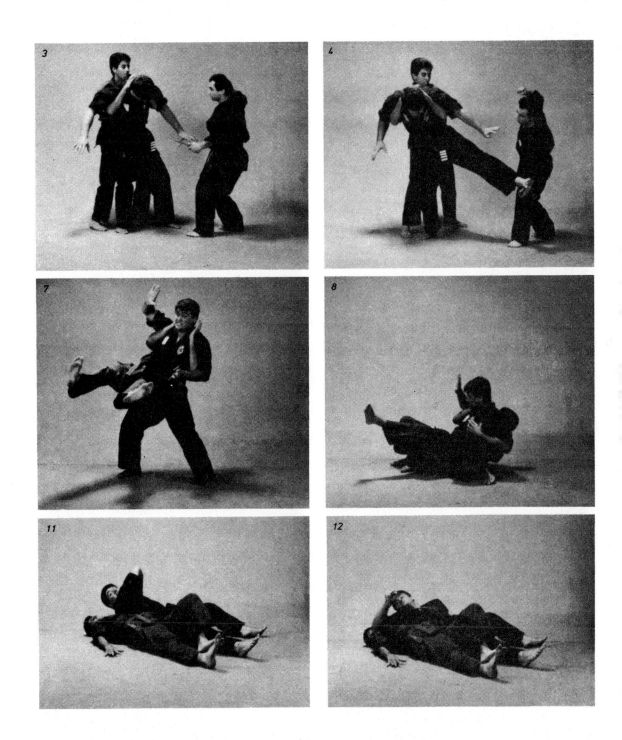

JAPAN

TRADITIONAL KARATE

Japan is unique in that it has many different martial arts and not one overall root art. The major form of combat practiced by Japan's warrior class was generically referred to as jujutsu (zhu-zhootsoo), also spelled jujitsu or jiujitsu.

Jujutsu evolved into various arts, such as aikijutsu, judo and aikido. There were many other weapons arts, such as iaido, kenjutsu, etc.

Off the south of Japan lies a chain of islands known as the Ryukyu islands, the largest of which is Okinawa. Since the Okinawans were a fierce and independent people who were subject to frequent invasion by Chinese and Japanese, they practiced a form of unarmed combat known simply as "te" (hand art). In the late 18th century, several voyages to China were made, and Okinawan fishermen and farmers were given the opportunity to learn Chinese kung-fu techniques.

These techniques were incorporated into the te schools and refined to meet the Okinawans' specific needs, and the art of karate (China hand) was born.

Early in the 20th century, an educator named Gichin Funakoshi brought karate to the Japanese mainland. Largely through the efforts of Funakoshi, karate became a rage in Japan, and spread throughout the world. It became so identified with Japan that the *kanji* (letters) were now read "empty hand," to eliminate identification with another nation.

Other arts of Japan: Aikido, Aikijutsu, Iaido, Judo, Jujutsu, Kendo, Kenjutsu, and Naginata-do.

Takayuki Kubota is one of the most highly ranked instructors of traditional Japanese martial arts in America.

1) Takayuki Kubota, perhaps the highest ranking traditional karateka in the United States, completely relaxes, clearing his mind of all preconceived notions and anticipations. 2) As his attacker punches, Kubota deflects the energy with an outside block. 3) He then punches his attacker's bicep insertion. 4) Kubota follows through with a backfist to the head. 5) A sweep kick to the inner thigh off balances the opponent. 6) The opponent is then easy prey for Kubota's elbow to the spine.

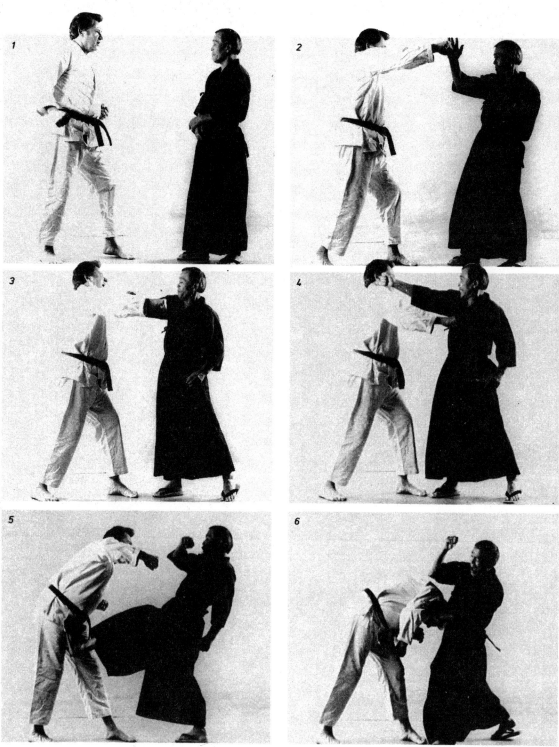

1) Soshihan Takayuki Kubota stands calmly as his opponent begins to kick. 2) He intercepts the kick before the opponent even extends with a reflexive downward block. 3) He closes the gap, delivering a left-cross to the opponent's jaw. 4) The opponent now stunned, Kubota grabs his lapels to gain control of him.

1) Soshihan Tak Kubota is gripped in a bear hug. 2) He breaks the hold by flowing his *ki* out through his fingers and bringing the arms up. 3) He traps the opponent's arms and slams back into the opponent's midsection with his buttocks. 4) Breaking the hold, he delivers a slap blow to the opponent's groin. 5) He pivots and off balances the attacker by grabbing the attacker's lapel. 6) The fight is ended with a blow to the base of the neck.

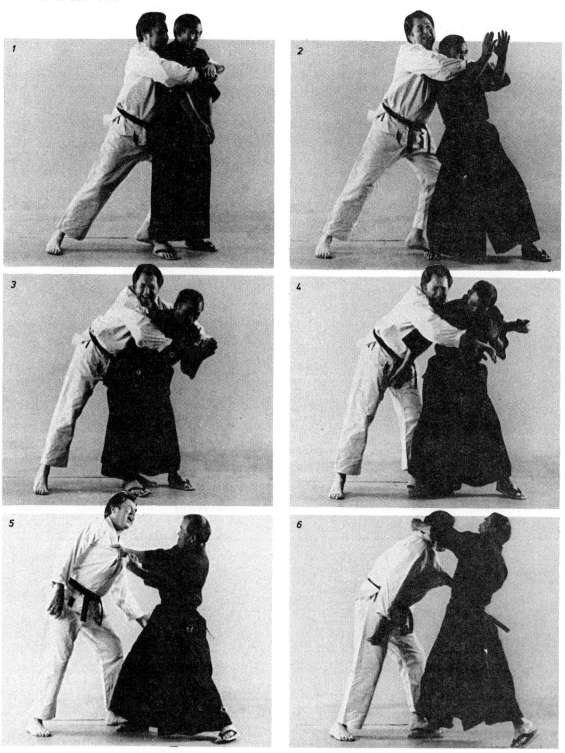

1) Soshihan Tak Kubota uses the motion of his fall to chamber his leg to kick. 2) He strikes forward in a side kick to the attacker's knee on the inside of the leg. 3) The attacker off balance, Kubota can now deliver a punishing kick to the attacker's midsection. 4) Kubota simply follows through with a force of the kick, knocking his attacker over.

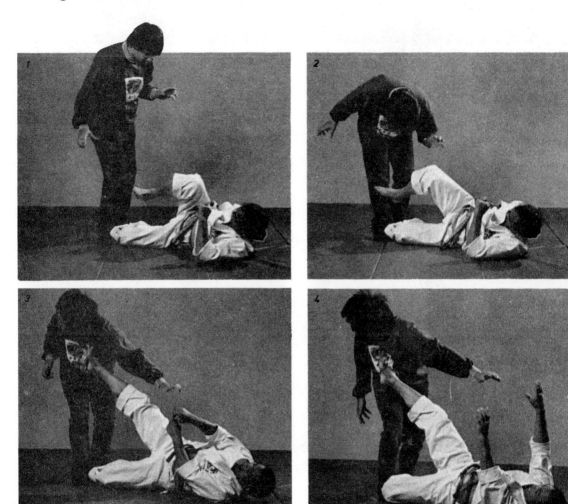

KOREA

TAE KWON DO

Korea lies between China and Japan, and, as such, has been subject to frequent invasions by both nations. Although the origins of Korean martial arts have been shrouded in mystery, two schools of thought have evolved. The first is that, at various times of occupation, the Koreans had the opportunity to learn both Chinese kung-fu and Japanese karate. The second is that the arts of Korea evolved independently. Most scholars believe the truth rests somewhere between the two stories.

Korean tae kwon do (tie kwon doe) is the most widely practiced martial art in the world today. It was the highlight of the 1988 Olympics. The art of tae kwon do, while a complete martial art, is characterized by a marked preference for fancy, acrobatic kicks.

Other arts of Korea: Hapkido, Tang Soo Do and Yudo.

Peter Lulgjuraj Is a tae kwon do Instructor who currently teaches in Southern California.

1) Peter Lulgjuraj, a black belt in tae kwon do and hapkido, faces his opponent. 2) Without warning, the attacker launches his punch, and Peter uses an outside reflex block. 3) Peter pulls the attacker's arm to him, and combines the attacker's momentum with his own as he steps in and delivers an elbow strike. 4) He then reaches behind his attacker's head, maintaining the trap on his hand, and grabs the back of his hair. 5) He steps around and twists, off balancing the attacker. 6) Peter's attacker is then thrown to the ground.

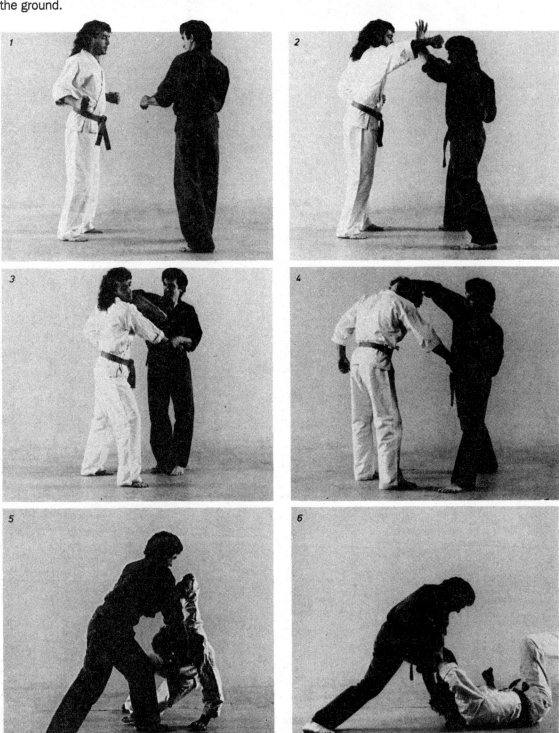

1) Peter Lulgjuraji faces an aggressive opponent calmly. 2) The opponent kicks and Peter reflexively steps to the side, out of the path of the attacking foot, and blocks the kick. 3) He steps in and fires a hard reverse punch into his opponent's now-open midsection. 4) Peter then follows up with a reverse roundhouse to the face. 5) Passing the opponent's face completely, he rechambers his kicking leg. 6) Peter finishes his foe with a hard roundhouse to the head.

KOREA

HAPKIDO

Another popular martial art in Korea is hapkido (hop Key doe). Hapkido was founded in the 1950's by Yong Suhi Choi, who had learned Daito Ryu aikijujutsu in Japan, and incorporated this knowledge with specialized Korean kicking and punching techniques. Hapkido utilizes strikes and grappling combinations, and is distinguished by the absence of forms.

Tae Man Kwon was one of the original students of Yong Suhl Choi, the founder of Hapkido.

1) Hapkido master Tae Man Kwon faces an attacker. 2) The attacker punches and Kwon parries. 3) Kwon turns around and grabs the attacker's wrist, and places his elbow up over the attacker's. 4) He simply levers the attacker to the ground. 5) Once the attacker is down, Kwon maintains the lock on the arm. 6) He continues the punishment with a blow to the face.

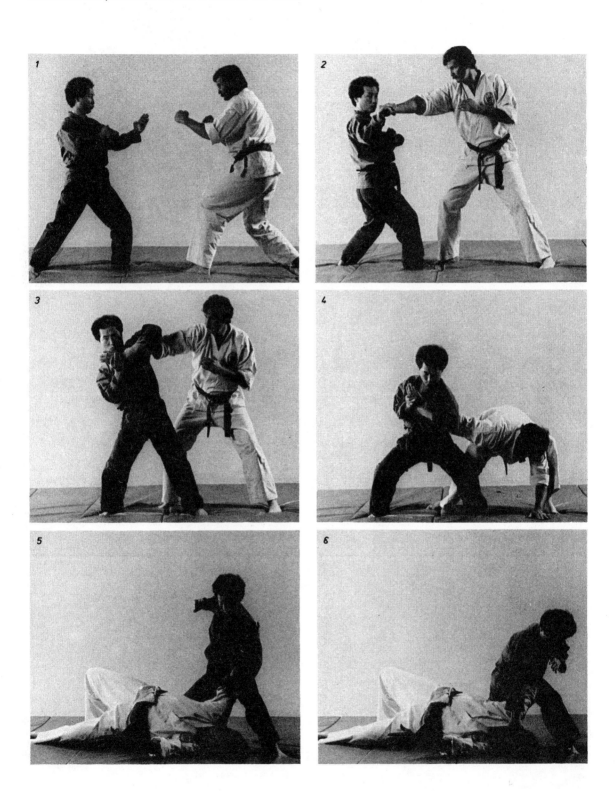

1) The attacker and Kwon face off. 2) The attacker chambers a kick, telegraphing his intentions. 3) Kwon traps the attacker's leg as the kick is launched. 4) He spins around and sweeps the attacker. 5) Kwon lands and jabs the attacker's eyes with his full bodyweight (6).

OKINAWA

KARATE

Okinawa is the largest of the Ryukyu Islands, a chain off of the coast of Japan. During the Middle Ages, the Ryukyu kings instituted repressive laws against the populace, outlawing the possession of weapons. As a result, the unarmed citizenry was easy prey for a hostile takeover by Japan.

During the occupation period, many fishermen made voyages to China, where they trained in Chinese kung-fu. This led to the development of shorin ryu (Shaolin school) karate, which served as a basis for the development of many other Okinawan styles. Many other systems, such as goju ryu and uechi ryu, evolved directly from various Chinese martial arts.

Adapting the Chinese arts to their own unique needs, such as using farm implements in place of illegal weapons, and hand conditioning techniques to smash through wooden armor, the Okinawans created what is today known as *karate* (China hand). There are numerous Okinawan systems including seidokan (formerly Motubu ryu), various styles of shorin ryu, isshin ryu, goju ryu, Okinawa kenpo, uechi ryu and kobudo (weapons).

Deborah Magone is a fourth dan sensei in Seidokan karate, formerly known as Motobu Ryu.

Deborah Magone stands facing her attacker (1), who suddenly aims a haymaker at her head, only to find his move simultaneously blocked and countered by a gouge to the throat (2). Continuing to rip his throat, Deborah chambers a kick (3), and kicks the back of his support knee (4). This takes him to the ground (5), and Deborah finishes him with a punch (6).

Deborah is about to become a victim (1), of the most common street attack (2). Unfortunately for her attacker, she suddenly delivers a powerful kick to his inner leg (3 & 4), which sends him sprawling (5). She can now finish him off with a kick (6).

Deborah faces her attacker, unaware of the hidden knife (1). As he thrusts, she turns at the waist, deflecting the knife with an upward parry (2). She sandwiches the knife hand between her hands (3), traps his hand while chambering around (4), twists hard at the waist, generating a tremendously powerful arm smash to the throat (5), and sweeps him down (6).

Deborah is attacked (1), and immediately turns her body to gain control (2). She knees the first attacker (3), side kicks the second (4), breaks and delivers an elbow strike (5), and turns to finish-off the first attacker (6).

Deborah isn't as helpless as she appears to be (1). Her attackers discover this as she stops one cold with a kick (2), and grabs the other by the arm (3). She leans forward, pulling the man up (4), and over (5), tossing him onto his companion (6).

Deborah assumes a neutral stance (1). As her attacker swings, she blocks (2), and grabs his hand (3). She twists him around, throwing her elbow over his straightened arm (4), then steps into a low stance, her bodyweight forcing him down (5). She finishes him by breaking his arm (6).

PHILIPPINES

KALI

When Ferdinand Magellan, at the beckoning of the king of Cebu, in the Visayan Islands of the Philippines, invaded the tiny kingdom of Mactan, he got more than he bargained for. The residents of Mactan, armed primarily with striking weapons, easily defeated the Spanish invaders with their martial art, known as arnis. Legend has it that Magellan met his death in a one-on-one duel with Lapu Lapu, the king of Mactan.

The most popular theory of origin is that Filipino martial arts, generally referred to under the umbrella term of kali, spread to the Philippines from Indonesia. There were many other inputs, such as the kuntao of the Moros in the south, and the incorporation of Spanish escrima (fencing) during the occupation period.

Ted Lucaylucay is certified as a full instructor of Filipino martial arts and jeet kune do concepts under Dan Inosanto.

1) Ted Lucaylucay, son of famed escrimador Lucky Lucaylucay, faces his attacker casually. 2) The attacker punches and Ted carefully controls his zone. Stepping back, so his body is out of the attacker's reach, he intercepts and attacks the punching hand with his elbow. 3) He then twists to the outside, angling, and elbows the nerve immediately above his attacker's elbow. 4) Ted grabs the attacking hand, raising it high, and pivots. 5) He continues the motion, twisting the attacker's hand around and forcing him to the ground.

1) Guro Ted Lucaylucay is grabbed. 2) He opens his arms wide, palms out, and rams his head back into his opponent's face. 3) He brings his left hand up high, breaking the pressure of the grip, and slashes to the opponent's groin with his right. 4) In a simultaneous move, he slaps down with his left, breaking the opponent's grip, and delivers a right uppercut. 5) He then breaks the hold with a double wristlock.

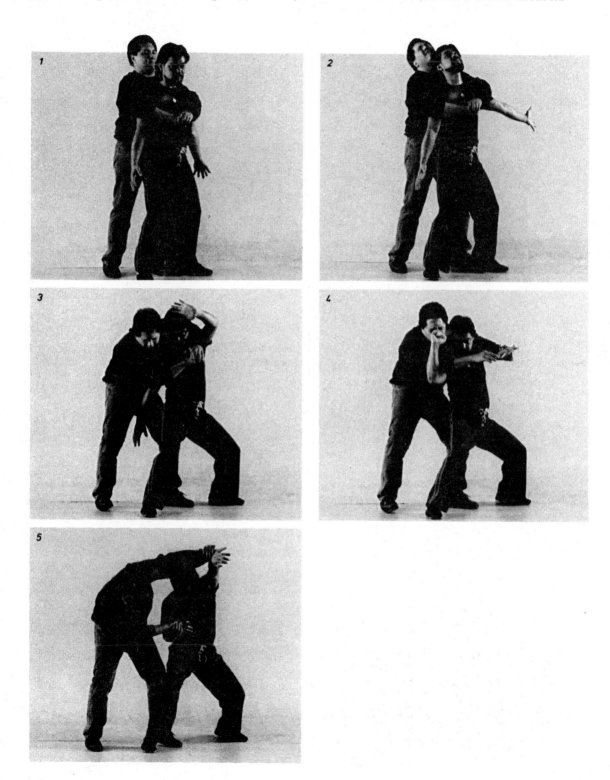

The brutal simplicity of Filipino martial arts is demonstrated by the brevity of these next two techniques. On this page, Ted is menaced by a knife-wielder (1). His opponent thrusts, coming into Ted's zone (2), and Ted ends the fight with one simple but sophisticated move as he steps out, traps down and thrusts (3).

On this page, Ted illustrates the double-check safety principle. The attacker faces him out of range (1). Again, when the attacker moves, Ted simultaneously angles out of the way, traps with his elbow and thrusts his knife (2). Although this theoretically would have ended the fight, Ted follows up by trapping and cutting down on the arm (3), and slashing across the midsection (4).

THAILAND

MUAY THAI

Thai boxers are the kings (and queens) of the ring. Thailand was once part of a vast empire, incorporating parts of Indonesia and the Philippines. It is speculated that Thai boxing was once a part of Indonesian silat. However, the fierce Thais developed it into an art of unparalleled power and brutal efficiency.

Thai boxers contend that it is not just their art which is so effective, for muay Thai is simplicity refined. It is, they insist, their training methods, consisting of grueling hours of practice in timing, precision and power development.

The primary arts of Thailand are muay Thai, ler drit—the military style of muay Thai—and krabi krabong, the Thai weapons art.

Willa Bell trained in muay Thai under such instructors as Nanfah Seharadecho, and became an active competitor in women's kickboxing until a promising career was sidelined by an injury sustained in an automobile accident.

1) Muay Thai is feared the world over for its brutal efficiency. Here, muay Thai student Willa Bell casually faces her attacker. 2) As the attacker moves, Willa, still not knowing what form of attack is to come, immediately raises her hands to her face, extending her elbows. 3) This both covers her, protecting her from the punch, and allows her to instantly counter with an elbow to the throat 4). She follows through with another elbow, this time to the face. 5) She next chambers her knee for a kick. (NOTE: The simplicity of muay Thai is such we broke the moves down into interim stages. The actual follow up took less than a second.) 6) She pulls her attacker into her powerful knee thrust.

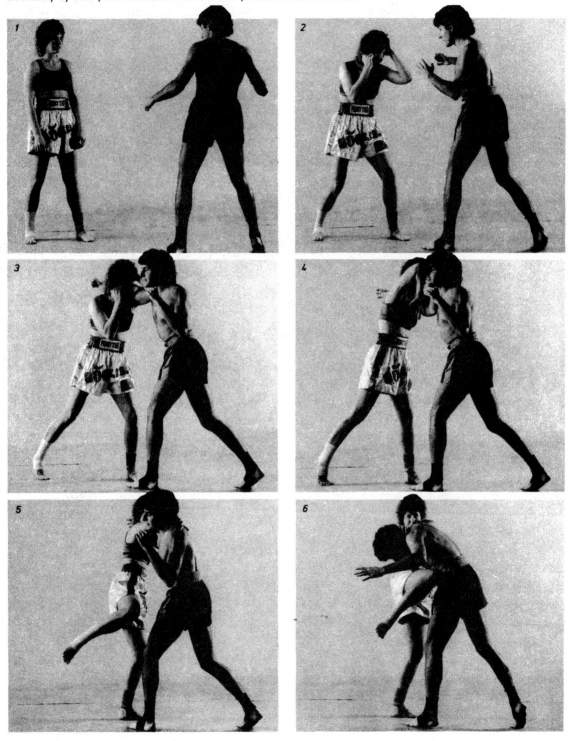

1) Muay Thai instructor Willa Bell is grabbed from behind. 2) She thrusts her head back into her opponent's face. 3) She steps to the side, bringing her left arm up and her right arm across her body, breaking the grip. 4) She slams her elbow into her opponent's midsection. 5) She then grabs her opponent behind his head and chambers her right leg. 6) She finishes him with a knee to the face.

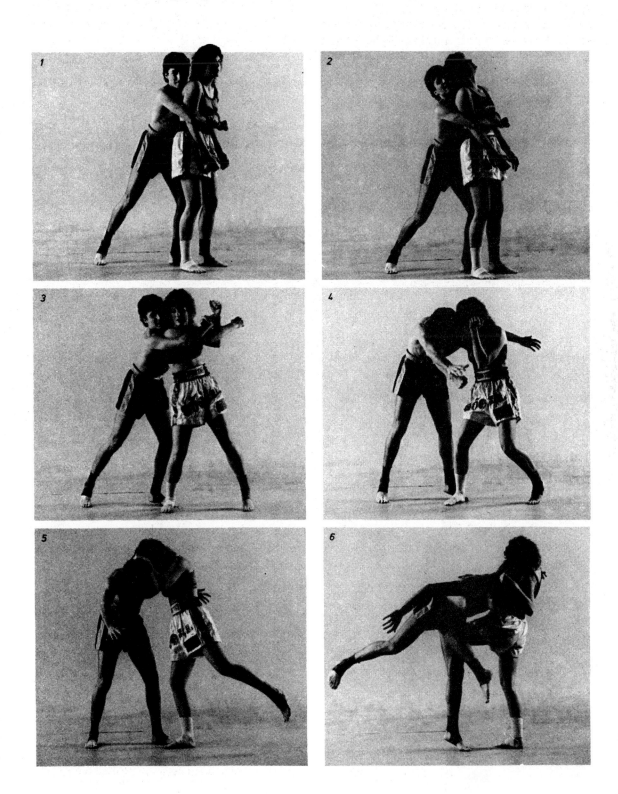

Nanfah "Lot" Seharadecho was the muay Thai champion of Thailand for five years running. He retired undefeated.

"Lot" faces off with his opponent (1), who launches his punch (2), and Lot intercepts it and delivers an elbow to the face (3), following it up with a knee to the midsection (4). Lot then wraps his opponent's neck (5), and delivers another punishing knee to the midsection (6). Once a Thai fighter has an opponent so "wrapped," it is common to repeatedly deliver punishing knee blows. This technique was so fast we had to break it down into its components.

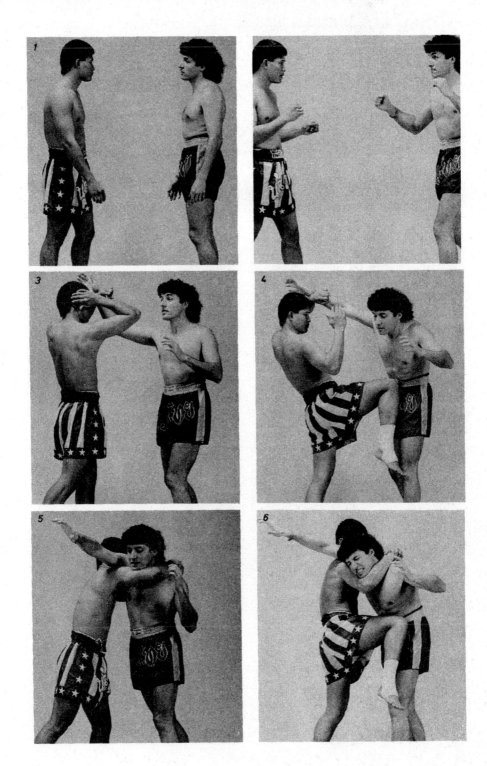

As the purse snatcher goes for Lot's gym bag (1 & 2), Lot instantly pivots and grabs the back of his head (3), knees him in the face (4), leaps for altitude (5), and smashes him on the back of the neck (6).

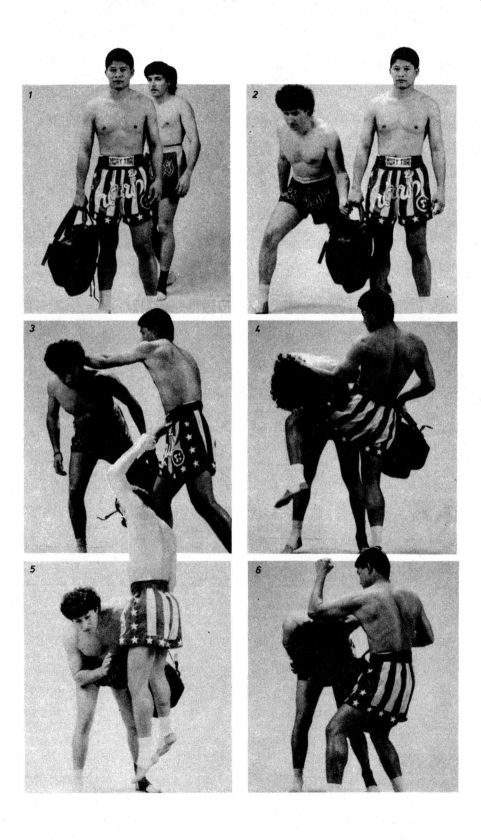

"Lot" faces his attacker (1), as he swings, Lot brings his elbow up (2), and leans in, hitting him (3). As the attacker reels, Lot brings his other hand around (4), and hits him with his other elbow (not shown) while pulling downward on his arm with his left elbow (5). Lot finishes by pulling the attacker into a fierce midsection knee (6).

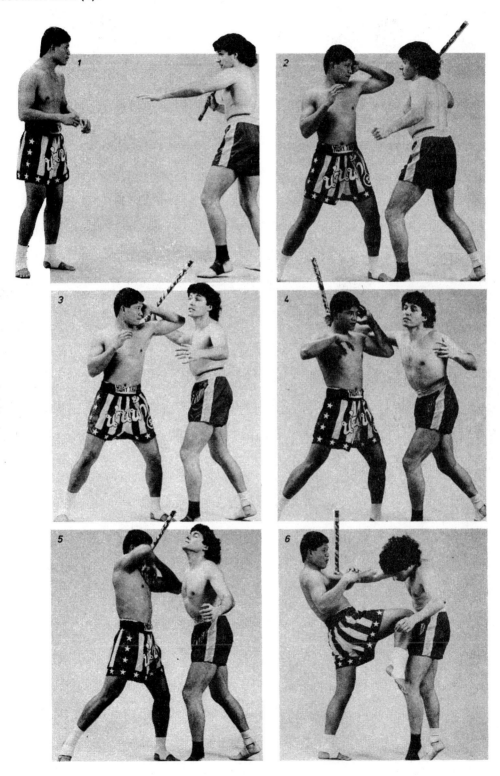

"Lot" faces his opponent, who has a knife hidden behind his back (1). Lot quickly sidesteps the thrust and pushes the knife with an underhand scoop (2). He flings the hand around so hard, the attacker loses his grab (3). Since Lot cannot presume the attacker lost the knife, he traps his hand downward (4), and cocks his elbow back. He delivers a powerful elbow strike to the temple (5), and a smashing hook kick to the abdomen (6).

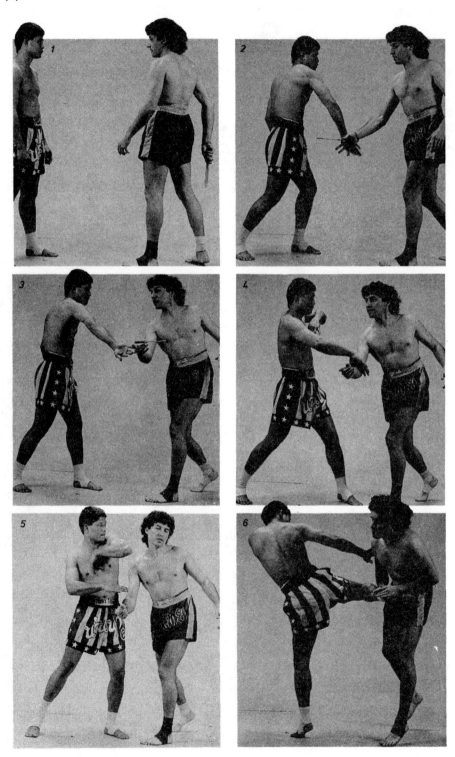

"Lot" finds his arms pinned (1). As the first attacker rushes, Lot holds him at bay with a kick (2), and head butts back (3). He thrusts a knee into the first attacker (4), and follows through with a punch (5). He pivots and finishes the attacker behind him with a knee (6).

Alfonso Tamez trained in ier drit and muay Thai in Bangkok. He is also a certified full instructor of jeet kune do concepts and Filipino martial arts under Dan Inosanto.

1) Alfonso raises into a defensive posture as his attacker launches a kick. 2) The attacker fires the kick and Alfonso "covers" his face and positions his weight evenly. 3) As the kick reaches Alfonso, he hits the inner part of his attacker's shin hard, with his elbows. 4) Immediately, he chambers his left elbow back. 5) Twisting his full body weight around, he strikes his opponent full force in the temple, and follows through, knocking him to the ground. 6) On the ground, he finishes him off by kneeing him in the head.

1) Alfonso faces his opponent. 2) As his opponent attempts a kick to his low-line, Alfonso simply sticks his foot out. 3) He meets the kick with a painful heel strike to the inner thigh, just above the knee. 4) He pushes down on the opponent's leg, forcing him to bring his foot to the ground. 5) Alfonso then leans forward and grabs the attacker behind the neck. 6) The attacker is finished as Alfonso steps up on his support leg and knees him in the face.

1) Alphonso Tamez moves forward as his opponent moves. 2) The opponent attempts a punch, which Alphonso sidesteps and blocks. 3) The opponent's motion carries him forward. 4) Alphonso immediately delivers a knee to the midsection. 5) This is instantly followed with another knee, in a "1-2" combination.

UNITED STATES

JAILHOUSE ROCK

Jailhouse rock is one of the newest and rarest forms of combat in the world. Basically, it is the stylized, organized fighting art of the Black American, developed in prison. Since, in prison, one's life could be in danger from a large group of assailants at any time, jailhouse rock is extremely effective against multiple attackers.

Dennis Newsome is one of the world's leading authorities on jailhouse rock and African martial arts.

1) Jailhouse rock was developed, in part, for instant responses in unexpected situations. Here, Dennis Newsome faces an attacker 2). As the attacker swings his fist, Dennis' hands instantly cover his face as he locks his hands behind his head. 3) Dennis now hits his opponent in the face with an elbow strike. 4) He repeats the move to the other side of the face in 1-2 fashion. 5) He follows the elbow moves with an upward strike to the groin. 6) The attacker is finished with a takedown.

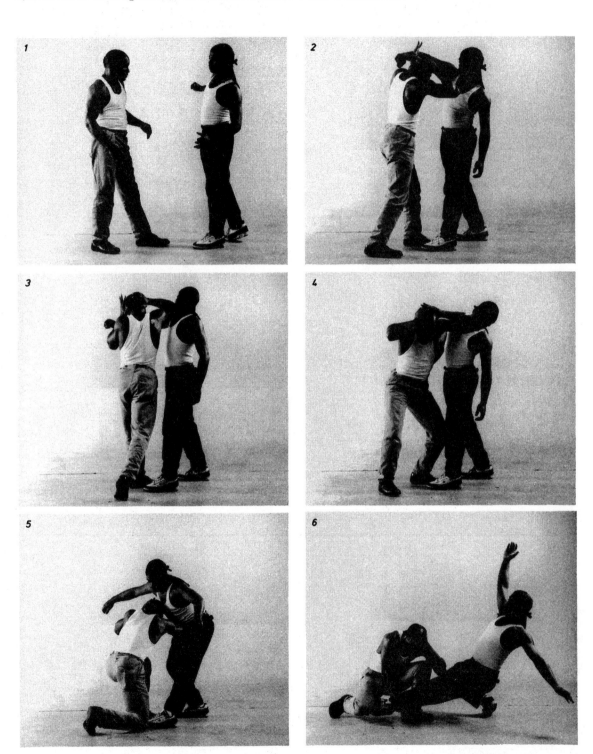

1) Dennis Newsome's guard comes up as he sees his opponent's foot move. 2) As his attacker kicks, he simultaneously knees and elbows the leg. 3) He quickly brings his foot forward, striking the back of his attacker's support knee. 4) He follows through with a strike to the face with the elbow as the attacker goes down. 5) On the ground, he drops on the attacker's groin. 6) The attacker is finished with an elbow to the face.

1) Dennis is grabbed from the back in a tight grip, his arms pinned. 2) He quickly brings his left arm up to relieve the grip. 3) Suddenly, he strikes the opponent's ribs with his elbow, while pulling himself free with his right hand. 4) He shoots his elbow up into the opponent's face. 5) Another followup blow with the other elbow is next. 6) A knee to the groin finishes the job.

1) Dennis Newsome is grabbed in a standard choke. 2) He quickly reaches up and strikes the left elbow with his left hand while grabbing his attacker's right fingers. This eliminates the pressure of the choke. 3) He begins to rotate and lower his body, at the waist. 4) Continuing the rotation frees him, while trapping both of the attacker's hands in Dennis' left hand. 5) Dennis finishes the job with an elbow to the face. 6) The attacker is knocked to the ground.

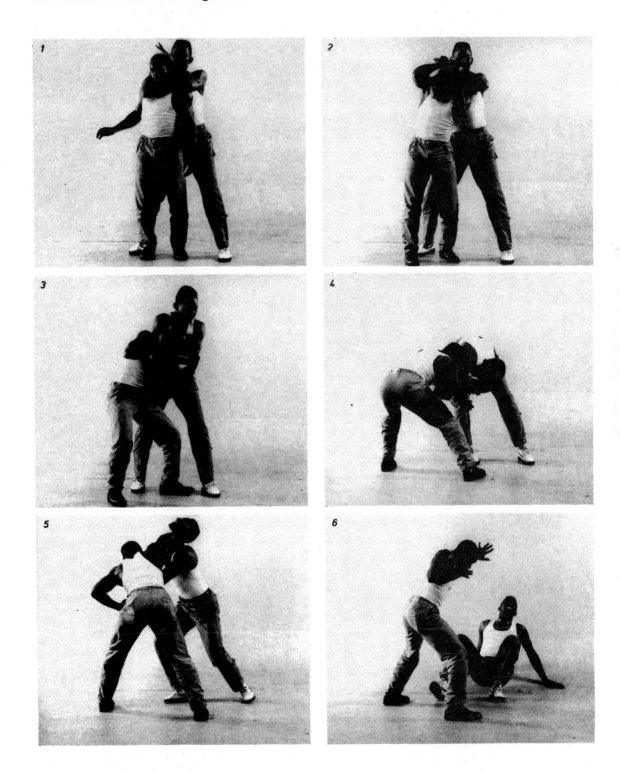

UNITED STATES

KARA-HO KENPO

Kara-ho kenpo karate is a uniquely American form. It was developed after World War II by William Kwai-sun Chow, based on kung-fu training from his father and various other arts to which he had been exposed. Chow resided in territorial Hawaii, which was relatively lawless in those days, and an attack could come at virtually any time. As a result, kara-ho is a brutal and instant system of defense.

Samuel Alama Kuoha is the current grandmaster of the kara-ho kenpo system, having inherited the leadership of the style from the late Professor William Kwai-sun Chow.

1) Samuel Kuoha, who learned kara-ho from his mentor, the late Professor William Kwai-sun Chow in Hawaii, casually faces an obviously menacing attacker, betraying no intent. 2) As the attacker punches, Kuoha drops into a crouch, his guard up to protect against a sudden kick or hand blow. 3) Sam shoots back up and traps the attacking punch and delivers an edge-of hand blow to the base of the nose. 4) He then shoots his fingers into the eyes. 5) An edge-of hand blow to the kidney follows. 6) The sequence continues with a kick to the inside of the knee.

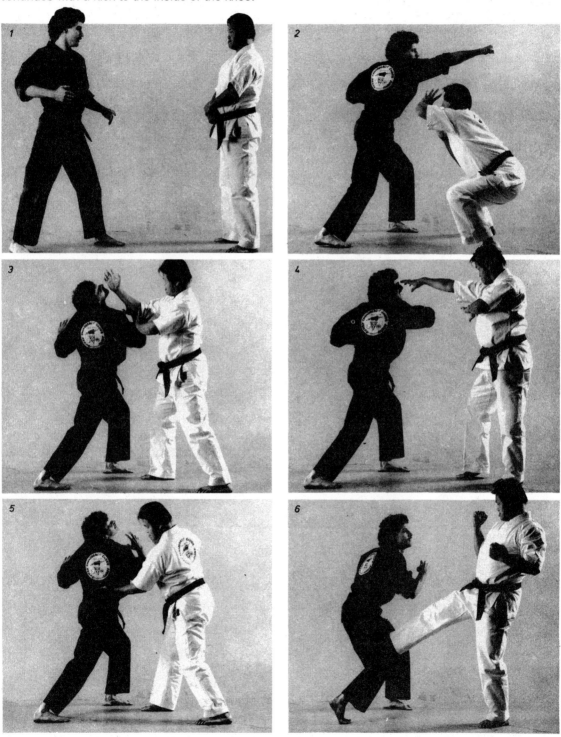

1) The instant he is grabbed, Sam brings his arms up to trap his opponent's arms, and fires a low line kick to the inside of the shin. 2) He grabs two of the attacker's fingers, pulling his hand loose, and fires an elbow to the ribs. 3) A palm heel to the throat finishes the fight.

Kenpo grandmaster Sam Kuoha stands next to his opponent (1). As his opponent launches a punch, Sam deflects the angle with an uppercut to the bicep (2), and locks the attacking limb (3). Maintaining the trap, he hammers the groin (4), delivers a cross to the face (5), and finishes with a takedown (6).

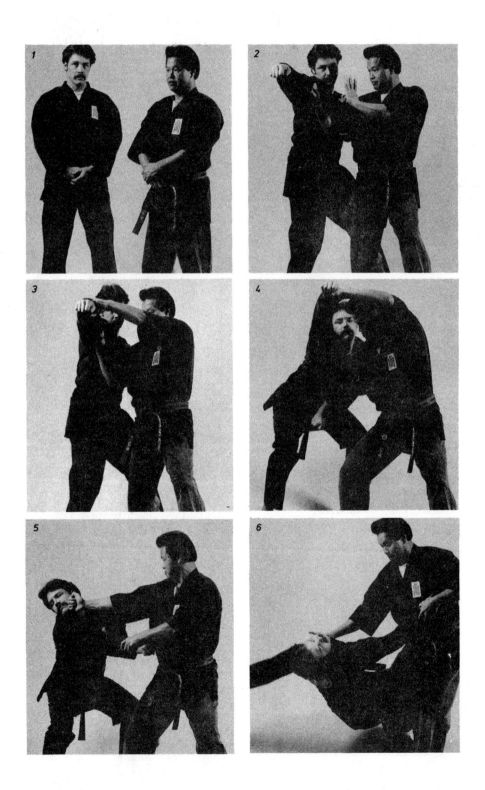

A thief sneaks up on his unsuspecting victim (1), and grabs his gym bag (2). Sam instantly bends him up and applies a lock (3), levers him down (4) to the ground (5), and applies a shuto to the neck (6).

While standing in a kara-ho preferred "innocent" stance, Sam is attacked (1). As the attacker swings, Sam snaps his body to the side and steps in with an intercept/arm break (2). He then fires a snap kick to the knee (3), knees to the head (4), and brings his leg over the back of his head (5). Bringing the attacker to the ground, Sam finishes him-off with an arm break (6).

Sam is grabbed by two men from either side (1). Instantly, he "kneecaps" one with a kick (2), and then thrusts a sidekick just below the knee (to the tendon) of the other (3). He then swings the same leg into a knee blow to the other man's face (4), thrusts a side kick into the remaining man (5), and spins around, finishing him off with a spin kick to the head (6).

Sam is grabbed by one and rushed by the other (1). He stops the rusher by impaling him with a thrust kick to the groin (2), and kicks the inside knee of the grabber (3). Sam then reaches down and grabs the right leg (4), pulling him off balance (5), and finishes off with a kick to the head (6).